Crowned

For Servant Leadership

Called. Chosen. Crowned.

To carry His Glory, Lead with Purpose, and

Finish the Work

Dr. Lisa M. Vice

Crowned for Servant Leadership

Copyright © 2025 Lisa M. Vice

Published by Martin Manor Publishing, P.O. Box 20, Katy, TX 77494

www.booksbylmv.net
Library of Congress Control Number: Pending

ISBN: 9798316292912

Printed in the United States of America
All rights reserved. No part of this publication may be reproduced, stored in a retrieval system, or transmitted in any form or by any means—for example, electronic, photocopy, recording—without the publisher's prior written permission. The only exception is brief quotations in printed reviews.

Unless otherwise indicated, Scripture quotations are taken from the New King James Version® Copyright © 1982 by Thomas Nelson. Used by permission. All rights reserved.
Scripture quotations marked CSB have been taken from the Christian Standard Bible®, Copyright © 2017 by Holman Bible Publishers. Used by permission. Christian Standard Bible® and CSB® are federally registered trademarks of Holman Bible Publishers.
Scripture quotations marked KJV are taken from the Holy Bible, King James Version, which is in the public domain in the United States.

Scripture quotations marked TPT are from The Passion Translation®. Copyright © 2017, 2018, 2020 by Passion & Fire Ministries, Inc. Used by permission. All rights reserved. ThePassionTranslation.com.

Scripture quotations marked (NIV) are taken from the Holy Bible, New International Version®, NIV®. Copyright © 1973, 1978, 1984, 2011 by Biblica, Inc.™ Used by permission of Zondervan. All rights reserved worldwide www.zondervan.com. The "NIV" and "New International Version" are trademarks registered in the United States Patent and Trademark Office by Biblica, Inc.™

Scripture quotations marked AMP are taken from the Amplified® Bible (AMP), Copyright © 2015 by The Lockman Foundation. Used by permission.
www.lockman.org.
Capitalization has occasionally been modified from the original.

Dedication

To Pastors Gbolahan and Margaret Faluade—
you are the kind of leaders heaven applauds.

You walk in the humility of Jesus,
serve with the heart of the Father,
and lead with the wisdom of the Spirit.

You have never sought the spotlight,
yet your light has guided many.
You have not built a ministry for fame,
but a people for God.

This book reflects the standard you have set—
one of character, sacrifice, obedience, and love.
You have lived the message I now write.

I dedicate this work to you, with deep gratitude and honor, believing your legacy will continue to raise up generations who lead like Christ, live like Christ, and love like Christ.

"The greatest among you will be your servant."
—Matthew 23:11 (NIV)

With all honor and blessing,
Dr. Lisa Michelle Vice

Crowned for Servant Leadership

Table of Contents

Introduction 7

Chapter 1 9
   The Call to Servant Leadership 9

Chapter 2 17
   The Fullness of the Holy Spirit and Wisdom 17

Chapter 3 23
   The Weight of the Crown 23

Chapter 4 33
   Humility: The Foundation of Leadership 33

Chapter 5 41
   True Recognition Comes from God 41

Chapter 6 49
   Community and Compassion: The Heart of Leadership 49

Chapter 7 57
   Unwavering in the Face of Opposition 57

Chapter 8 67
   Waiting on God's Timing 67

Chapter 9 75
   The Narrow Path of Servant Leadership 75

Chapter 10 83
   Carrying the Weight of Glory 83

Chapter 11 93
   The Fivefold Leader: Fulfilling Your Ministry Mandate 93

Prayer for the Finishers 101
About the Author 103

Introduction

A quiet stirring is happening in the hearts of believers across the world. In small prayer groups, in corporate boardrooms, and on bustling city streets, God is raising up an army—unseen by most, but undeniable in their calling. What if you were called to be part of God's final movement before His return? Would you be ready to step into your divine assignment?

The church stands on the threshold of a new and mighty move of God, and the time for preparation is now. As the prophetic and apostolic movements have paved the way, the Spirit of God has stirred the hearts of apostles and prophets to establish movements such as the Esther and Deborah Arise movement, which is currently taking shape. Armies are forming, tribes are gathering, yet the work remains unfinished. God is not yet satisfied.

The completion of this divine work is near, as the Spirit of the Lord continues to stir the hearts of His apostles and prophets to raise up a new generation of leaders. These leaders are called to rise and step into their divine appointments. In hindsight, former moves of God have seen measures of compromise, but this generation of servant leaders is set apart—they are the uncompromised ones. They are the finishers who will bring forth the completion of God's work on earth before His return.

At the same time, God is awakening His people, and the call to arms is resounding. Believers are being summoned. Now is the time to rise—no room for hesitation. The world is waiting for the display of God's glory through these leaders, and the season of preparation is drawing to a close.

On April 9, 2024, I received a word from the Lord that He is calling those who, like Stephen in Acts 6, are positioned with the character of servant leaders. Stephen was one of the seven appointed to complete the work of a servant leader. Today's Stephens are those who will finish and perfect the work of God.

This new generation of leaders—men and women alike—will rise in the Spirit. **Called** and **Chosen** by God, affirmed by peers, and appointed by mentors, they will carry their calling beyond the church into businesses, professions, and communities. These adults will walk as Stephen did, full of faith, the Holy Ghost, and power. They are ***Crowned*** for servant leadership. Through them, God will reveal Himself to the world as they carry and display the knowledge of His glory (*Habakkuk 2:14*).[1]

In the chapters that follow, we will examine the parallels between Stephen's role and the leadership of those being called today.

The world is waiting to receive from these leaders, chosen for such a time as this. They are called to step up and step into their divine purpose, showing forth the light they carry. They must heed the call, embrace the charge, and emerge from the secret place to bring hope and redemption to nations, churches, and the world through the manifestation of God's glory.

The call to action is clear. As darkness covers the earth,[2] the time to respond is now. Step up, answer the call, and prepare for the brightness of your light to shine!

Chapter 1
The Call to Servant Leadership

The call to servant leadership has never been more critical than it is today. Modern-day Stephens—men and women marked by humility, faithfulness, and the power of the Holy Spirit—are rising to fulfill God's divine purpose. These individuals, like Stephen in the book of Acts, are crowned with both victory and responsibility, called to lead through service and sacrifice.

The Four Traits of a Modern-Day Stephen

Every servant leader God calls carries four distinct traits:

1. Humility – Like Christ, they lead not for personal gain but through sacrificial service. (*Philippians 2:5*)

2. Faithfulness – They remain steadfast, even in trials, knowing their work is unto God. (*Psalm 23:4*)

3. Holy Spirit Empowerment – Their strength is not their own; they are led and filled by the Spirit. (*Acts 6:8*)

4. Marketplace Influence – They extend their leadership beyond church walls, impacting businesses, schools, and communities.

These four traits set them apart. As you read the stories that follow, ask yourself: Which of these traits do I already carry? Which do I need to develop?

Innocence and Humility in Servant Leadership

The modern-day Stephen embodies innocence and humility, living as Christ did. *Philippians 2:5*[3] calls us to have the same mindset as Jesus: a servant who humbled Himself to the point of death. This humility is the cornerstone of their leadership, allowing them to serve selflessly and with great compassion.

Psalm 23:4*(NIV)* reminds us, "*Even though I walk through the darkest valley, I will fear no evil, for you are with me; your rod and your staff, they comfort me*." The Stephens of today walk through challenges with unwavering faith, knowing God is their source of strength and guidance. Their humility shines in the way they prioritize others, reflecting Christ's love.

Servant Leadership: Contentment and Purpose

Could you be a modern-day Stephen? True servant leaders don't seek recognition—they find joy in serving. What if your greatest impact is hidden in your daily obedience? Their lives are defined by stewardship, focusing on the needs of the community rather than personal gain. As servant leaders, they carry out God's work with an eternal perspective, understanding the weight of their calling.

The life of Stephen in the New Testament illustrates this perfectly. Though chosen to serve tables, he performed his duties with excellence, full of faith and the Holy Spirit. This faithfulness opened doors for God to use him in greater ways, even to the point of performing signs and wonders among the people (*Acts 6:8*).[4]

Empowered by the Holy Spirit

The defining trait of modern-day Stephens is their empowerment by the Holy Spirit. They are equipped with wisdom, grace, and courage to face opposition and to carry out their mission. This empowerment enables them to rise above fear and remain steadfast in their calling, even in the face of adversity.

Their reliance on the Holy Spirit sets them apart as leaders who are not moved by external circumstances but led by divine guidance. It is this dependence that allows them to be vessels of God's glory, impacting lives both inside and outside the church.

Marketplace Apostles and Prophets

In addition to spiritual leaders, modern-day Stephens include marketplace apostles and prophets—those called to carry God's presence into secular spaces. These individuals serve as bridges between the church and the world, demonstrating Christ's love and truth in their professions.

Marketplace apostles lead with integrity, exemplifying God's principles in business and society. Prophets in the marketplace speak boldly, bringing light to dark places and reminding others of God's sovereignty. Together, they extend the Kingdom of God beyond church walls, fulfilling the Great Commission in diverse contexts.

Sarah, David, and Maria's Stories

In a vibrant urban neighborhood marked by both opportunity and struggle, a group of humble servant leaders rose to meet the needs of their community. They didn't carry titles of prominence, yet their work reflected the spirit of modern-day Stephens—faithful, Spirit-filled, and steadfast in their service. Each one, guided by the Holy Spirit, operated uniquely as marketplace apostles and prophets, blending ministry and profession to bring transformation.

Sarah: The Prophetic Educator in the Classroom and Beyond

Sarah, a schoolteacher with a prophetic edge, was sensitive to the spiritual and emotional needs of her students and their families. Growing up in a family committed to prayer and community service, Sarah had learned early on how to hear the voice of the Holy Spirit. While her job as an educator required discipline and structure, Sarah also saw it as her ministry. She often prayed over her lesson plans, seeking divine wisdom to reach the hearts of her students.

One evening, as Sarah sat exhausted at her desk, she felt the weight of her students' struggles. A single mother confided in her about losing her job; another child hadn't eaten in two days. 'God, how do I reach them?' she whispered. As she prayed, a plan formed in her heart—one that would change not just test scores, but lives. She began organizing after-school programs that incorporated not only academic tutoring but also emotional and spiritual support for children and their parents. Speaking prophetically into their lives, Sarah identified gifts and talents in the children that even their parents hadn't recognized. By blending education with prophetic insight, she equipped the next generation to rise above their circumstances and pursue God's calling.

David: The Apostolic Builder in the Marketplace
David had spent forty years in construction, hands calloused from years of laying brick and driving nails. Retirement should have been a time to rest, yet his spirit was restless. He couldn't ignore the growing number of homeless families in his city—mothers and children huddled in doorways, young men sleeping on park benches.

One morning, as he knelt in prayer, a clear vision flashed before him: abandoned buildings transformed into sanctuaries of hope. He heard the words in his heart, "Rebuild not just walls, but lives."

Doubt crept in. "God, I'm just one man. What can I do?" Yet, the burden didn't lift. With trembling faith, he made a few phone calls—to former colleagues, church leaders, city officials. Slowly, doors opened. What started as a single project turned into a city-wide movement.

David's apostolic gifting came alive as he organized teams, negotiated with city officials, and inspired volunteers. Under the Spirit's guidance, he developed partnerships with local businesses and churches, rallying support and resources for his projects. Each building became more than just a shelter; they were hubs of restoration where individuals could find hope, mentorship, and community. David didn't just build shelters; he restored dignity. Men and women who had lost everything now had a place to rebuild their lives. Where the world saw ruins, God had seen a future.

David's leadership demonstrated how marketplace apostles could bridge the gap between business and ministry, creating practical solutions while advancing God's Kingdom.

Maria: The Visionary Advocate and Marketplace Prophet

Maria had grown up watching her mother struggle—juggling two jobs, stretching every dollar. She knew what it was like to go without. It was these early hardships that fueled her passion for justice. But as a college student, she often felt powerless.

"God, I want to help, but where do I even start?" she prayed one evening.

Then, the vision came. A gathering. Not just another charity event, but a place where businesses, churches, and nonprofits could unite to empower, not just assist. Job training. Counseling. Resources. Hope.

Fear whispered: You're just a student. No one will listen to you. But faith shouted louder. She reached out—to professors, community leaders, even local businesses. To her surprise, they believed in her vision.

Months later, as she stood in a packed auditorium, watching lives change, she realized: God didn't need her status. He just needed her yes. Her studies and her faith worked hand in hand as she sought to bring both systemic change and spiritual renewal.

Maria's prophetic gifting allowed her to see potential where others saw obstacles, and her event became a catalyst for ongoing collaboration between the marketplace and the church. Her work revealed how marketplace prophets can speak God's truth and align diverse entities for His purposes.

A Unified Mission
Though Sarah, David, and Maria came from diverse backgrounds, their shared reliance on the Holy Spirit brought cohesion to their efforts. Together, they embodied a ministry that seamlessly integrated with the marketplace, addressing both spiritual and practical needs.

Sarah's prophetic insight empowered families to see beyond their immediate struggles. David's apostolic leadership built tangible structures that restored dignity and community. Maria's vision united resources and opportunities to bring lasting change. As they worked together, the Spirit wove their distinct callings into a cohesive tapestry of service and transformation.

This modern-day team of Stephens reminds us that servant leadership isn't confined to traditional ministry roles. It thrives in classrooms, construction sites, and boardrooms. By embracing the guidance of the Holy Spirit, marketplace apostles and prophets can bring God's Kingdom into every sphere of life, creating a ripple effect of change that glorifies Him.

A Call to Action

God is calling you now. Will you step up? Will you surrender fear and step into your divine appointment? The world is waiting. Heaven is watching. Your time is now. God is seeking those who will serve with humility, empowered by His Spirit, to carry out His work in this generation.

You, too, can be crowned for servant leadership. Like Stephen, commit to walking in faith and obedience, trusting that God will equip you for every good work. Your service will not only transform lives but also bring glory to God.

Reflection and Meditation

1. Reflect on the traits of modern-day Stephens (*Acts 6*)—humility, faithfulness, and Holy Spirit empowerment. How can you embody these in your daily life?
2. Meditate on Philippians 2:5 and ask the Lord to align your mindset with that of Christ.
3. Identify one area where you can serve with greater contentment and purpose this week.

As you ponder these questions, may the Lord guide you to live as a modern-day Stephen, crowned for His glory and ready to lead through service.

Chapter 2

The Fullness of the Holy Spirit and Wisdom

What does it mean to be full of the Holy Spirit?

The early church was marked by believers who didn't just have a touch of the Spirit—they were filled with Him, saturated, empowered to move in wisdom, faith, and miracles. Stephen, one of the first deacons and martyrs of the faith, exemplified this fullness. But how does one attain it? How do we become like Stephen—full of faith, power, and wisdom?

The journey to fullness is not instant; it is a process of transformation. Stephen did not start as a man full of glory—he became one through faith, obedience, and intimacy with God. His story is not just an ancient account—it is a roadmap for us today.

The Fullness of the Holy Spirit: A Process, Not an Event

Many believe that being filled with the Holy Spirit happens in a single, dramatic moment. While encounters with God are real and powerful, the fullness we see in Stephen was cultivated through process and obedience.

Take David Wilkerson, for example, a small-town pastor who became a global evangelist. He was not instantly full of power and boldness—he was simply obedient to a small nudge from the Holy Spirit to go to New York City and minister to gang members. That single act of obedience led to the birth of Teen Challenge, a ministry that has transformed millions of lives. His fullness grew as he obeyed God, step by step.

Obedience: The Key to Maintaining Fullness

Luke 4:1 tells us:

***"And Jesus, being full of the Holy Ghost, returned from Jordan and was led by the Spirit into the wilderness**.*"

Notice the order:

1. Jesus was filled.

2. He was led.

3. He was tested.

This is the pattern for fullness. Every person God fills, He leads. And where He leads, there will be testing.

Have you ever felt like God led you into a wilderness season right after a breakthrough?

Perhaps you experienced a powerful encounter with God, only to face unexpected opposition or hardship.

Maybe you stepped out in faith, only to be met with doubt, rejection, or delays.

Do not be discouraged. Testing is proof of fullness. The same Spirit that led Jesus into the wilderness also led Him out in power (*Luke 4:14*).

Stephen's Journey to Fullness: A Result of Intimacy with God

The Bible says Stephen was full of faith and power, doing great wonders among the people (*Acts 6:8*). But how did he get there?

Consider a young David tending sheep. He didn't start as a mighty warrior—he was a worshipper first. Alone in the fields, David built intimacy with God. This hidden time of worship and trust prepared him to face Goliath in power and faith.

Two Key Takeaway:

1. Fullness is cultivated in the secret place.

2. Public power is a result of private intimacy.

How is your secret place with God?

Biblical Examples of Fullness: A Life of Power.

Throughout Scripture, we see people full of the Spirit move in extraordinary power:

- The 120 in the upper room – Filled at Pentecost, preaching with boldness (*Acts 2:4*).[5]
- Peter – Once timid, now preaching fearlessly, full of the Holy Spirit, boldly addressed the rulers (*Acts 4:8*).[6]
- Stephen – Operating in wonders and signs (*Acts 6:3, 5, 8*).[7]
- Paul – Confronting demonic opposition (*Acts 13:9*).[8]

- Micah – Declaring truth with unshakable boldness (*Micah 3:8*).[9]

Modern-Day Stephens: God is Raising You Up

A Prophetic Call:

Today, God is raising up modern-day Stephens—men and women willing to walk through the fire, endure the process, and carry His glory into the world.

Many want the power, but few embrace the process. Will you?

Reflections:

1. What areas of your life is God calling you to surrender to His process?

2. Are you allowing Him to lead, even into wilderness seasons?

3. Are you cultivating private intimacy so you can walk in public power?

Activation:

1. Spend time in prayer, asking God to reveal any areas of resistance in your heart. Surrender them to Him and invite the Holy Spirit to take full control of your life, guiding your thoughts, actions, and decisions.

2. Set aside intentional time each day to deepen your relationship with God through worship, prayer, and meditating on His Word. Ask Him to fill you with His

presence and wisdom, allowing His fullness to transform your daily walk.

3. Identify one step of faith or act of obedience God is prompting you to take—whether in your personal life, ministry, or leadership. Commit to acting on it this week, trusting that obedience opens the door to greater spiritual fullness.

Declaration:

May you walk boldly through the process, trusting that God's work in you is leading to the fullness of His Spirit and wisdom. The filling is not an end—it is a means to reveal His glory. The path may be narrow, but it is filled with eternal significance.

Crowned for Servant Leadership

Chapter 3
The Weight of the Crown

Throughout history, crowns have symbolized authority, honor, and sovereignty. But in Scripture, crowns hold a deeper meaning—representing divine purpose, spiritual victory, and eternal rewards.

From the crown of thorns to the crowns of righteousness, rejoicing, and glory, each carries a profound truth about leadership, sacrifice, and perseverance. Understanding these crowns equips us to lead with wisdom, endure trials, and align our calling with God's purpose.

The Crown of Divine Purpose

1 Peter 5:4 (NIV) reminds us:

"And when the Chief Shepherd appears, you will receive the crown of glory that will never fade away."

Leadership is not about status—it is about serving God's purpose. Just as a crown encircles the head, God's calling surrounds every aspect of your life, shaping your decisions and guiding your leadership journey.

Personal Revelation: A Crown Named "Faithful"

There was a time when I wrestled with self-doubt, questioning whether my work had any real impact. Late at night, alone in my prayer room, I whispered my frustrations to God.

Crowned for Servant Leadership

"Am I making a difference, Lord?"

As I sat in the stillness, something unexpected happened. In my spirit, I saw a vision—a golden crown descending toward me. As it rested on my head, I noticed a single word inscribed on it: "Faithful."

Tears welled in my eyes. God wasn't measuring my leadership by numbers, applause, or titles—only by faithfulness.

The crown didn't come after the victory. It didn't arrive once the work was complete, or the audience was convinced. It came *in the middle* of my wrestling, while I was still pouring out my heart in quiet obedience. God was not waiting until I crossed a finish line to affirm me—He was with me *in the process*, acknowledging the unseen labor, the private surrender, the daily "yes" no one else heard.

I sat there for a long time, overwhelmed—not because I had done something great, but because I had simply been *seen*.

That moment shifted everything.

In today's world of performance and comparison, the crown of divine purpose reminds us that obedience, not recognition, aligns us with God's eternal plan.

The vision of that crown didn't just comfort me. It commissioned me.

From that day forward, I stopped asking, "Am I enough?" and started praying, "Lord, help me remain faithful—whether seen or unseen."

And I believe He's saying the same to you.

You don't need to be validated by men when you've already been crowned by God.

Stay the course. Finish the race. *Be faithful.*

The Crown of Glory

This crown is given to those who lead with humility, perseverance, and a servant's heart. It is not about gaining influence but about pointing others to Christ.

Personal Revelation: When No One Sees

There was a season in my leadership journey when I felt completely overlooked. I was serving faithfully—pouring into people, handling responsibilities—but it seemed no one noticed.

One night, exhausted, I sat before God. "Lord, does any of this even matter?"

In the quiet of that moment, I felt Him whisper: "Not one act of service goes unseen."

I was reminded that true leadership is not about visibility, but about faithfulness. Each unseen sacrifice builds toward an eternal reward.

The crown of glory calls us to embrace leadership not for human recognition, but for God's glory alone.

The Victor's Crown

James 1:12 (NIV) declares:

"***Blessed is the one who perseveres under trial because, having stood the test, that person will receive the crown of life that the Lord has promised to those who love him.***"

Leadership is not for the faint of heart. Whether in the church, the marketplace, or your community, walking in divine purpose means you will inevitably face trials—moments that test your resolve, challenge your identity, and stretch your faith.

Some trials feel like fire.

For the young leader who feels unseen while watching others get promoted, the trial is **rejection**. For the mother working two jobs and still answering the call to ministry, the trial is **exhaustion**. For the business owner building with integrity while competitors cut corners and prosper, the trial is **discouragement**. For the prophetic voice being misunderstood or silenced, the trial is **isolation**.

Add to that the silent battles: **financial strain, spiritual warfare, betrayal by those you trusted**, or even the quiet ache of **waiting on a promise that hasn't come to pass**.

These are not small things. They wear on the soul. They tempt us to question whether God sees us, whether obedience is worth it, and whether we're truly making a difference.

But then—James reminds us.

Blessed is the one who *perseveres* under trial. Not the one who avoids it. Not the one who escapes it. But the one who stays the course, walks through the fire, and comes out refined—not because they were strong, but because they refused to give up.

The victor's crown isn't for the perfect—it's for the persistent.

The crown of life is for the one who chose to worship through weeping, to serve when it wasn't convenient, to speak truth when it wasn't popular, and to keep showing up even when no one noticed.

And that might be you.

You may be in the middle of a storm right now—feeling pressed on every side. But I want you to know: *God sees your perseverance.* Every time you said "yes" when it would've been easier to quit, heaven was watching. Every time you prayed when you could've complained, believed when you had no reason to, and blessed someone else while you were bleeding—God was keeping count.

He is not unjust to forget your labor of love (*Hebrews 6:10*).
There is a crown on the other side of this trial.

And it's not just a reward—it's a reminder.
That your love for Him was real. That your obedience mattered. That your trial wasn't wasted.
That everything you endured prepared you to carry greater

glory, greater authority, and greater compassion for the people you're called to serve.

So keep going.

Hold the line.
Stand your ground.
You are not losing—you are lasting.
And those who last receive the victor's crown.

Personal Revelation: Confronting the Black Bull

It was one of the most intense spiritual battles of my life. I felt a relentless heaviness pressing against me—discouragement, fear, and a sense of unworthiness. One night, I had a vision.

I found myself standing in an open field when suddenly, a massive black bull appeared. Its fiery red eyes locked onto me, nostrils flaring, ready to charge. I knew immediately—it was a representation of the enemy's intimidation.

For a moment, fear gripped me. But then, something shifted. Authority rose up within me. With boldness, I stepped forward, lifted my hand, and declared, "In the name of Jesus, you have no power here!"

Instantly, the bull's horns shattered, its sight darkened, and it stumbled backward into the shadows. As it disappeared, I felt a weight settle on my head—a crown. And in my spirit, I heard God's voice: "Go serve."

That moment changed everything. Victory in the spiritual realm equips us to take new ground for God's kingdom.

Leadership is not just about standing your ground—it's about advancing God's purposes.

The Crown of Righteousness

2 Timothy 4:8 (NIV) speaks of this crown:

"Now there is in store for me the crown of righteousness, which the Lord, the righteous Judge, will award to me on that day—and not only to me, but also to all who have longed for his appearing."

This crown is for leaders who refuse to compromise. In a world that rewards shortcuts, true leadership stands on integrity and faithfulness to God's principles.

Personal Revelation: Choosing Integrity Over Success

Years ago, I faced a defining moment. A shortcut was presented to me—one that would have fast-tracked success but required me to compromise my values.

Everything in me wrestled. The opportunity looked good on paper, but in my spirit, I felt unrest. I knew what God was asking of me, yet the temptation was strong.

After much prayer, I made my choice—I walked away. The road was harder, longer, but it was clean. And in time, God honored that decision with peace, provision, and greater opportunities that required no compromise.

The crown of righteousness is a reminder: It is always better to obey God than to chase quick success.

In today's culture, these moments of decision come in many forms—signing a partnership with someone whose ethics don't align with yours, manipulating numbers to keep a contract, softening your convictions to stay popular, or remaining silent when God calls you to speak. The pressure to succeed can blur the line between strategy and compromise. But righteousness calls us to draw a line in the sand and say, *"I belong to God, and I will not sell my integrity for influence."*

You have the power to choose well—not by willpower alone, but by leaning into the strength of the Holy Spirit. Prayer will anchor you when temptation pulls. God's presence will sharpen your discernment and strengthen your resolve. And when you choose integrity, even in secret, heaven sees it. And heaven rewards it.

Stay faithful. Your crown is forged in private obedience. And what God has for you will never require you to betray who He made you to be.

The Crown of Rejoicing

1 Thessalonians 2:19 (NIV) describes this crown:

"*For what is our hope, our joy, or the crown in which we will glory in the presence of our Lord Jesus when he comes? Is it not you?*"

This crown is about investing in people. True leadership is not about accolades—it's about lives transformed.

Personal Revelation: The Greatest Reward

I will never forget the day I received a message from someone I had mentored years ago.

"You may not remember this," they wrote, "but a conversation we had changed my life. You saw something in me that I couldn't see in myself. I wouldn't be where I am today without that moment."

I was stunned. I had forgotten the conversation, but God had used it to plant a seed that bore fruit in someone else's life.

That's when I realized: The greatest reward of leadership is not what we build—it's who we build.

Reflections:

1. Which crown resonates most with your current leadership journey?

2. How have trials shaped your leadership, preparing you for greater purpose?

3. Who in your life represents your "crown of rejoicing"—someone whose growth has been impacted by your leadership?

Activation:

1. Pray and ask God which crown He is refining in you right now.

2. Write a declaration about your leadership—one that aligns with God's eternal perspective.

3. Reach out to someone you've mentored or encouraged and affirm their growth.

Final Thoughts

The crowns you bear as a servant leader are not just symbols of authority—they are reminders of your divine calling.

Each challenge, victory, and act of service is shaping your eternal legacy. Leadership is both a privilege and a responsibility, requiring humility, boldness, and perseverance.

Embrace the weight of the crown. Lead with purpose, perseverance, and joy—advancing God's kingdom with every step.

Chapter 4
Humility: The Foundation of Leadership

Leadership is a journey, and humility is its foundation. In this chapter, we explore how trials, adversity, and self-reflection forge humility within leaders, preparing them for the responsibilities of servant leadership. Using the story of Joseph as a guide, we'll discover how past experiences shape character and how true greatness is achieved not through power or status, but through service and grace.

Joseph's Journey: A Model of Humility

Joseph's story in the Old Testament exemplifies the refining nature of humility. Betrayed by his brothers, sold into slavery, and unjustly imprisoned, Joseph endured immense suffering. Yet, he remained steadfast in his faith and humility.

Through these trials, Joseph's character was shaped. His journey from the pit to the palace teaches us that humility is not born from comfort but forged through hardship. When he finally rose to power in Egypt, Joseph demonstrated grace, wisdom, and forgiveness, prioritizing service to others over personal revenge or self-promotion.

Personal Reflection:

I remember a season in my life when I faced unexpected betrayal. People I trusted turned away, and I found myself alone, questioning my purpose. At first, I was consumed with frustration, but over time, I realized that God was using that isolation to refine my heart. I learned to lead not from a place of pride but from a posture of surrender. Like Joseph, my greatest growth came in the unseen moments—when no one was watching, and all I had was my faith.

Key Takeaway: Humility in leadership is not merely an attitude—it is a strength built through adversity. Reflect on Joseph's example as you face your own challenges, trusting that God uses these experiences to prepare you for greater purposes.

True Leadership: Serving with Humility and Grace

In a world that often equates leadership with dominance and authority, servant leadership offers a countercultural perspective. True leadership prioritizes serving others over self-promotion, embodying humility, and grace in every interaction.

Grace, as defined *in Strong's Concordance (G5485)*, emphasizes the capacity given by God to fulfill one's calling. In *Acts 6:8*, Stephen, one of the first deacons, exemplified this grace. Though his role differed from the apostles', Stephen operated with the same capacity to fulfill his calling. This reveals an important truth:

> **It is not the title or position that defines a leader but the grace and capacity to fulfill the work.**

Regardless of your role—whether in ministry, business, or your community—the capacity to serve others remains constant. Leadership is not about asserting superiority but about faithfully fulfilling your assignment with grace.

Practical Application:

Consider how you can embody humility and grace in your leadership. Are you leading for recognition, or are you serving to uplift and empower those around you?

Spiritual Foundations: Building on the Work of Others

Leadership does not occur in isolation; it builds upon spiritual foundations established by others. Stephen's effectiveness as a leader was rooted in the discernment of the prophets and the foundational work of the apostles.

This principle applies today. Leaders, like present-day Stephens, rely on the spiritual insights and foundational teachings of others. Collaboration and interdependence strengthen the leader's ability to serve effectively.

Personal Reflection:

I once had a mentor who invested time in me when I was just beginning my journey. Her wisdom, encouragement, and patience laid a foundation I still stand on today. Now, as I lead others, I realize I am not building something new—I am continuing the work of those who came before me.

Key Takeaway:

Humility in leadership acknowledges the contributions of others and recognizes that no leader stands alone. As you lead, seek wisdom from mentors, peers, and spiritual leaders, allowing their guidance to enrich your own work.

Reflecting on Past Experiences

Every leader has a journey filled with triumphs, setbacks, and lessons. Reflecting on your past experiences reveals how trials have shaped your character and leadership style.

Joseph's Example: His trials equipped him to lead with wisdom and compassion. In the same way, your challenges can prepare you to lead with humility, empathy, and grace.

Personal Reflection:

There was a moment when I faced public criticism in leadership—unfair, unexpected, and deeply personal. I remember the sting of words spoken without understanding, the sideways glances, and the subtle distancing of those I thought stood with me. My first instinct was to defend myself, to fight back, to prove my worth and clear my name. The temptation to set the record straight burned hot in my chest.

But instead of handing me a script for retaliation, God handed me silence.

He led me to *listen*—not to the voices of accusation, but to His. In the quiet place, He asked me, *"Do you trust Me to be your defense?"* It was there, in the hidden place of surrender, that I learned one of the hardest truths of leadership: **humility is not silence out of weakness— it is restraint out of strength.**

Humility meant choosing growth over ego. It meant letting God shape my character rather than protect my image. But even more, it meant releasing the right to be right, and instead choosing **mercy** over revenge.

It would have been easy to gather my receipts, to point out flaws in those who spoke against me. But God reminded me that leadership in His Kingdom doesn't destroy—*it restores*. Mercy doesn't mean we deny the wound; it means we choose to heal without inflicting another.

In that season, God refined me in the fire of misunderstanding. And though it hurt, I came out clearer, lighter, and more compassionate. That moment reshaped how I lead today. I no longer lead to be validated—I lead to be **faithful**. I no longer need to win battles of opinion—I fight to preserve the unity of the Spirit in the bond of peace (*Ephesians 4:3*).

> *True leadership isn't proven in defense—it's revealed in how we respond to offense.*

And when we choose humility over pride, mercy over revenge, and growth over vindication, we walk the narrow road with Jesus Himself—who, even when falsely accused, opened not His mouth (Isaiah 53:7).

Practical Insight:

The greatest leaders are those who have faced adversity and emerged not hardened, but softened—ready to lead with a heart of service.

Reflections:

1. What past experiences have shaped your leadership style?

2. How can you cultivate a greater posture of humility in your leadership?

3. Who in your life has helped lay a foundation for your growth as a leader? How can you honor and acknowledge their influence?

Activation:

1. Spend 5–10 minutes in prayer or journaling, asking God to reveal areas where He is cultivating humility in you. Write down any insights or convictions that arise.

2. Identify one person who has played a significant role in your leadership journey. Reach out to them this week with a message, note, or conversation expressing gratitude.

3. Choose one situation where you would normally assert your leadership or take credit, and instead, step back. Allow someone else to lead, and intentionally support them from behind the scenes.

4. Identify one act of service you can do this week without announcing it—whether in your home, workplace, or community. Let this be a practice in leading through quiet strength rather than public acknowledgment.

5. Find a mentor, spiritual leader, or accountability partner who can speak into your leadership journey. Ask them to pray with you and hold you accountable for walking in humility and grace.

Final Thoughts

The journey of humility is a lifelong process, shaped by trials, reflections, and intentional growth. Like Joseph, you may find yourself in seasons of adversity, wondering about your purpose. Yet, it is through these moments that God prepares you for leadership rooted in service, compassion, and grace.

True greatness is not about ascending to power; it is about descending to serve. As you lead with humility, remember that your past experiences have equipped you for this moment, and your influence will leave a legacy far greater than any title or accolade. Trust in God's guidance, and embrace the journey with faith and courage.

Chapter 5
True Recognition Comes from God

The applause fades. The accolades diminish. The titles shift. But one truth remains unshaken: true recognition comes from God.

It's easy to crave validation from others—to measure success by applause, likes, promotions, or titles. But leadership in the Kingdom isn't about being seen by the crowd; it's about being known by God. When we truly grasp that our calling is ordained by Him, we stop chasing recognition and start walking in divine confidence.

This chapter explores the difference between human validation and God's affirmation. Through the stories of Jeremiah, David, Hannah, and Jesus Himself, we'll uncover how real leadership is forged—not in the spotlight, but in the secret place where God's approval is enough.

The Source of Our Calling

Imagine a young man, trembling at the weight of a calling too great for him. Jeremiah wasn't looking for a title. He wasn't striving for leadership. Yet, before he was even born, God had already chosen him.

"Before I formed you in the womb I knew you; before you were born I sanctified you; I ordained you a prophet to the nations." —Jeremiah 1:5 (NKJV)

Jeremiah tried to resist. ***"I am too young,"* he protested. *"I don't have the words."*** But God interrupted his doubt: ***"Do not say, 'I am a youth,' for you shall go to all to whom I send you, and whatever I command you, you shall speak."*** — ***Jeremiah 1:7*** (NKJV)

Jeremiah's story is a reminder that our calling is not about our qualifications—it's about God's purpose. When He calls, He equips. When He appoints, He anoints. We don't have to prove ourselves. We just have to trust Him.

Key Insight:

Just as God knew Jeremiah's destiny before he was born, He has ordained your leadership for His purposes. Rest in the assurance that your calling originates from Him and is sustained by His grace.

True Recognition Comes from God

In today's world, driven by likes, shares, and accolades, it's easy to fall into the trap of seeking validation from others. However, Scripture reminds us that true recognition comes from God. He sees beyond outward appearances and measures the intentions of our hearts.

Consider David. When Samuel was sent to anoint Israel's next king, he assumed the strongest, tallest, most experienced son would be the chosen one. But God had a different perspective:

"Do not look at his appearance or at his physical stature, because I have refused him. For the Lord does not see as man sees; for man looks at the

outward appearance, but the Lord looks at the heart." —1 Samuel 16:7 (NKJV)

David, the shepherd boy, overlooked and underestimated, was the one God had chosen. His anointing wasn't based on appearance, charisma, or human validation. It was rooted in God's plan.

Even Jesus didn't seek recognition from people. His ministry didn't begin with public accolades—it began with the Father's voice:

"This is My beloved Son, in whom I am well pleased." —Matthew 3:17 (NKJV)

Jesus didn't need the Pharisees' approval or the crowd's applause. His identity was secure in the Father.

What about you? Are you leading for recognition, or are you leading because God called you?

Key Insight:

Pursue a heart of integrity and faithfulness, trusting that God will affirm and validate your efforts in His perfect timing. When God is pleased, no human approval is needed.

Embracing Your Identity as Chosen Vessels

Titles fade. Positions change. But your identity in Christ remains.

"But you are a chosen generation, a royal priesthood, a holy nation, His own special people,

that you may proclaim the praises of Him who called you out of darkness into His marvelous light." —***1 Peter 2:9*** (NKJV)

Jesus, the King of Kings, washed the feet of His disciples. He humbled Himself to the point of death on a cross. His leadership wasn't about self-promotion—it was about servanthood.

When you understand that you are chosen by God, you stop striving for validation and start serving with confidence.

Jeremiah faced opposition. He was rejected, persecuted, and ignored. But God reassured him:

"They will fight against you, but they shall not prevail against you. For I am with you," says the Lord, "to deliver you." —***Jeremiah 1:19*** (NKJV)

No amount of rejection can cancel what God has ordained.

Key Insight:

When your foundation is in God, you are unshaken by human approval or criticism.

A Story of Divine Recognition: Hannah's Legacy

Hannah knew what it felt like to be overlooked.

In ancient Israel, a woman's worth was often measured by her ability to bear children. Hannah, unable to conceive, faced years of scorn from her rival, Peninnah. The whispers, the humiliation, the judgment—it was relentless. (*1 Samuel 1:10-11*).[10]

One day, overwhelmed with grief, Hannah went to the temple to pray. She wept before God, pouring out her anguish.

"Lord Almighty, if you will only look on your servant's misery and remember me... then I will give him to the Lord for all the days of his life." —*1 Samuel 1:11* (NIV)

Eli, the priest, saw her lips moving but heard no sound. He assumed she was drunk.

"How long will you be drunk? Put your wine away from you!" he scolded (*1 Samuel 1:14* (NKJV).

Imagine the sting of that accusation. Here she was, seeking God with all her heart, and she was misunderstood—even by a priest. But Hannah didn't react in anger. She responded with humility, explaining her anguish.

God saw her heart. And in His perfect timing, He answered her prayer. Hannah gave birth to Samuel, a prophet who would anoint kings.

Her recognition didn't come from society—it came from God.

Key Insight:

Like Hannah, entrust your efforts and desires to God, knowing that He sees your faithfulness and will honor it in His perfect timing.

Reflection and Activation

1. Set aside time this week to pray specifically about your calling. Ask God to reveal His affirmation over your life and leadership, and surrender any need for human approval to Him.

2. Identify one area where you've been seeking recognition from others—whether through titles, achievements, or approval. Make a conscious decision to shift your focus toward pleasing God rather than people.

3. Take one bold step this week in your leadership journey—whether speaking up, serving someone in humility, or stepping into a new opportunity—trusting that God has already validated you.

Final Thoughts

True recognition comes not from applause, promotions, or social validation—it comes from God. When you embrace this truth, you stop striving and start leading with confidence. You no longer chase approval. You walk in purpose.

As you move forward in your leadership journey, let *Galatians 1:10* be your foundation:

Crowned for Servant Leadership

"For do I now persuade men, or God? Or do I seek to please men? For if I still pleased men, I would not be a bondservant of Christ." —Galatians 1:10 (NKJV)

Trust in the One who called you. His recognition is eternal, His timing is perfect, and His plans for you are greater than anything the world can offer.

Chapter 6
Community and Compassion: The Heart of Leadership

The weight of leadership is not measured in power but in service. True leaders do not stand above their people; they walk beside them. Their influence is not dictated by titles but by the lives they touch.

At the heart of effective leadership is community and compassion. A leader who understands this fosters a culture of trust, humility, and shared purpose. In a world that often elevates personal ambition over collective well-being, servant leadership stands as a bold and countercultural act—one that mirrors the very heart of Christ.

This chapter explores how leaders cultivate genuine relationships, lead with compassion, and navigate challenges with grace. And, as we will see in Thomas' story, a leader's greatest legacy is not built in moments of ease, but in times of adversity.

Cultivating Genuine Relationships

A leader is only as strong as the relationships they build. Leadership is not about issuing commands but walking with people, understanding their struggles, and lifting them up. Jesus exemplified this perfectly—He ate with the outcasts, comforted the broken, and called His followers not just servants, but friends.

In John 13:34-35 (NKJV), He commands:

"A new commandment I give to you, that you love one another; as I have loved you, that you also love one another. By this all will know that you are My disciples, if you have love for one another."

Genuine relationships are built in the quiet moments: a leader who listens when no one else does, who notices the unspoken burdens on someone's shoulders, who shows up when it matters most.

Key Insight:

Trust is the currency of leadership. When people feel seen and valued, they invest themselves fully in the vision.

Leading with Compassion

Compassion is the mark of a servant-leader. It is the ability to look beyond oneself and into the hearts of others. ***Matthew 9:36*** (NKJV) paints a vivid picture of Jesus' compassionate leadership:

"But when He saw the multitudes, He was moved with compassion for them, because they were weary and scattered, like sheep having no shepherd."

Great leaders don't just see problems—they see people. They recognize pain beneath the surface, discouragement behind forced smiles, exhaustion hidden behind duty. Compassion compels action. It steps in when others step away.

> ***A leader's strength is measured not by their authority, but by their ability to lift others when they have nothing left to give.***

Key Insight:

Compassionate leadership creates an atmosphere of belonging, empowering others to grow and thrive under your care.

Navigating Challenges with Grace and Humility

Leadership is tested in hardship. Conflicts arise. Expectations go unmet. Pressures mount. But a leader's response in these moments defines their impact.

Philippians 2:3 (NKJV) offers a radical perspective on leadership:

"Let nothing be done through selfish ambition or conceit, but in lowliness of mind let each esteem others better than himself."

True leadership is not about defending one's ego—it is about seeking wisdom, admitting mistakes, and choosing grace over pride. Humility does not weaken a leader; it strengthens them.

> **Grace and humility are essential for navigating leadership challenges. They allow leaders to remain grounded, approachable, and effective in times of difficulty.**

Key Insight:

A leader who leads with humility creates a culture of trust and unity, even in times of conflict.

Thomas' Story: A Legacy of Community and Compassion

Thomas grew up in a valley where the mountains met the sky, a place where everyone knew each other's names and hardships. His father's words echoed in his mind from childhood:
"We are blessed to be a blessing."

His family lived modestly, but their home was always open—to the hungry, the weary, and the brokenhearted. From a young age, Thomas understood that leadership was not about status but service.

A Divine Calling

As he grew, Thomas felt a pull toward ministry—not behind a pulpit, but among the people. He found his purpose in a struggling community center, its walls cracked with age, its rooms empty except for broken chairs and fading hope.

Where others saw ruins, Thomas saw potential. He envisioned a place where children could learn, families could heal, and the weary could find refuge. He poured his time, energy, and meager resources into restoring it—one small act of faith at a time.

Proverbs 3:27 (NKJV) guided his steps:
"Do not withhold good from those to whom it is due, when it is in the power of your hand to do so."

Over time, the center became a beacon. It housed job-training programs, food drives, and mentorship circles. Thomas never sought recognition, only transformation.

A Test of Faith

Then, the flood came.

The river swelled under relentless rain, and within hours, the village was drowning. Homes were lost. Livelihoods washed away. Fear gripped the community.

Thomas had nothing to offer but his presence—but sometimes, presence is **everything**.

Standing in the wreckage of what was once a village square, he rallied the people:
"We will rebuild together. No one stands alone."

Galatians 6:2 (NKJV) became their rallying cry:
"Bear one another's burdens, and so fulfill the law of Christ."

With whatever they could salvage, they rebuilt. The center became a shelter. The broken found healing. Hope was no longer a concept—it was a reality they created together.

Thomas' leadership was never about his own strength. It was about his willingness to trust God's.

A Legacy of Transformation

As weeks turned into months, the village began to recover. Homes were rebuilt, crops replanted, and hope restored. Through Thomas' leadership, the community not only survived but became stronger. Villagers who had never worked together before found unity in their shared purpose.

Thomas' impact extended far beyond the immediate crisis. He taught the villagers the power of compassion, selflessness, and faith. His leadership inspired others to step into their own roles as servant-leaders, ensuring that the legacy of community and compassion would endure for generations.

In the years that followed, the community center became a symbol of hope, a place where lives were transformed through the love of Christ. Though Thomas never sought recognition, his story spread, inspiring others everywhere to embrace servant leadership.

Key Insight:

Thomas' story reminds us that true leadership is rooted in compassion, charity, and faith. Even in the face of overwhelming challenges, a servant-leader can transform lives and communities by trusting in God's guidance and prioritizing the needs of others.

Reflection and Activation:

1. Think of someone you lead—how can you strengthen your connection with them this week? Take one step to show intentional care.

2. Identify a quiet need in your community or team that often goes unnoticed. How can you meet that need in a way that reflects God's heart?

3. Consider a leadership challenge you're currently facing or recently navigated. Ask God for wisdom, and choose one way to respond with humility rather than control.

4. Write a personal prayer asking God to help you lead through connection, not position. Ask for a renewed heart to serve those around you with patience and love.

5. Just like Thomas, look for a situation that requires not just leadership but presence. Show up where others hesitate. Be the example others need to see.

Final Thoughts

Community and compassion are the heart of servant leadership. By building genuine relationships, leading with empathy, and navigating challenges with grace, leaders create environments where others can thrive.

Thomas' story reminds us that true leadership is not about personal glory but about uplifting others and reflecting God's love. As you continue your leadership journey, remember the words of **Colossians 3:12** (NKJV): ***"Therefore, as the elect of God, holy and beloved, put on tender mercies, kindness, humility, meekness, longsuffering."***

Lead with love. Serve with humility. And trust that God will use you to transform lives—one act of compassion at a time.

Chapter 7
Unwavering in the Face of Opposition

You never truly know the strength of your calling until it's tested.

Every servant leader will one day come face-to-face with resistance—not just from the world, but from systems, people, and spiritual forces that stand in direct opposition to the work God has called them to do.

There comes a moment in every leader's journey when silence is no longer an option.
When obedience costs you comfort.
When your calling invites resistance.

And the only thing left to do—
is stand.

Whether in a courtroom, a boardroom, or the stillness of your prayer closet, this moment tests more than your skills. It tests your conviction.

Do you truly believe what you say you believe? Will you still lead when no one claps? Will you still speak when your voice shakes?

Servant leadership isn't forged in applause—it's forged in fire.

What do you do when standing for truth makes you a target? When obedience leads to accusation? When you're outnumbered, misunderstood, and spiritually outmatched?

You stand.

You stand like Stephen.
You stand like Emily.
You stand like the countless faithful who refused to bow to fear—and in doing so, changed the world around them.

Stephen's Example: Unshaken in the Fire

The first martyr of the New Testament wasn't a man of political power or public fame. He was a deacon—humble, Spirit-filled, chosen to serve.

He stood before men who hated him.
Religious elite with stones in their hands.
Accusers twisting his words.
A crowd demanding silence.

Stephen's heart pounded, not with fear—but with fire.

"Now Stephen, a man full of God's grace and power, performed great wonders and signs among the people." —Acts 6:8 (NIV)

But miracles stir both faith and fury.
Opposition rose.
False charges flew.
The Sanhedrin's eyes narrowed.

Still, Stephen didn't back down. With every word, he testified boldly—anchored not in eloquence, but in the Holy Spirit. His face, Scripture says, shone like an angel's. He wasn't afraid. He was full.

Full of power.
Full of grace.
Full of God.

And when they dragged him outside to kill him, he still stood—this time in intercession.
"Lord, do not hold this sin against them."

Stephen's body fell.
But his courage lives on.

Key Insight:

The power to lead under pressure doesn't come from natural boldness. It comes from supernatural filling.

The Hidden Crown

It's easy to admire the strength of spiritual heroes from afar. But what happens when *you* are the one placed on the frontlines?

What if your assignment leads straight into a hostile workplace, an indifferent church, a broken system?

Let me tell you what it's like.

My Story: Light in a Dark Place

I didn't ask for the assignment.
But God promoted me anyway.

One day I was an employee. The next, I was managing a facility with one hundred fifty people—many of them wounded, addicted, angry, or spiritually bound. The darkness in the atmosphere was almost tangible.

At first, I thought the resistance was about leadership changes. But no—this was spiritual.
Grievances rolled in. Accusations flew. Some days, it felt like I was bleeding quietly behind a smile.

One night, I broke down in prayer.
"Lord, did You send me here just to suffer?"

And in the silence, I felt Him whisper:
"I didn't send you there to suffer. I sent you there to shift."

That night, I changed how I showed up. I was in a war.
Each morning, I declared Scripture aloud in my car.
I walked the halls before others arrived, speaking peace into every corner.
I laid hands on empty chairs, praying for healing and deliverance.

And slowly—miraculously—it began.

One employee overcame addiction.
Another reconciled with her husband.
A department known for dysfunction began to unite.

God was moving—not because I had it all together, but because I *surrendered to the shift.*

Key Insight:

Opposition isn't always a sign to retreat. Sometimes, it's the sign you've been sent to reclaim enemy territory.

Ephesians 6:12 (NIV) declares: *"For our struggle is not against flesh and blood, but against the rulers, against the authorities, against the powers of this dark world and against the spiritual forces of evil in the heavenly realms."* **Armed with this truth, I leaned on the Holy Spirit for strategy, prayed fervently, and walked in God's authority.**

Spirit-Led Leadership: Your Greatest Weapon

Jesus—the Son of God—never made a move without the Holy Spirit.

"The Spirit of the Lord is on me…" —Luke 4:18 (NIV)

He didn't just lead by divine nature. He led by divine *dependence*.

If Jesus needed daily communion with the Spirit—how much more do we?

During that season of intense warfare, I learned to *lead on my knees*. Not a day began without prayer. Not a decision was made without seeking wisdom.

I asked the Holy Spirit for strategy, not just comfort. And in response, I received both.

Key Insight:

The Holy Spirit doesn't just empower your voice—He sharpens your vision. He reveals what others miss and equips you to lead where others fail.

Emily's Story: Standing for Justice

She stood on the steps of city hall—papers in her hand, prayers in her heart. The same town that raised her now stood divided.

Emily had returned home with a degree in public policy and a heart full of purpose. But not everyone welcomed her mission.

Her goal was simple: to bring equity to a town long shaped by injustice. She launched a grassroots coalition—advocating for education, housing, job training.

But resistance came fast.
Board members called her naïve.
Officials ignored her proposals.
Even local media twisted her words.

One reporter sneered in a live interview, "What makes you think a twenty-something can fix a system generations old?"

She smiled, steady-eyed.
"Nothing about me. But everything about the God who sent me."

When the cameras turned off, her team huddled in prayer.
One of them read from **_Galatians 6:9_**:
"Let us not grow weary in doing good..."

They didn't.

Emily worked behind the scenes—mentoring teens, counseling single moms, rewriting policy with faith leaders and civic organizers.

And it paid off.

A housing bill passed.
A workforce program launched.
A new community center opened—this one named after her grandfather, a man who once picked cotton in that same county.

Her story made headlines. But it wasn't the media that defined her. It was the fruit.

Key Insight:

When you're led by conviction—not applause—your legacy outlives your leadership.

Key Takeaway:

Emily's journey reminds us that servant leadership is not without challenges, but perseverance, faith, and humility have the power to bring lasting change.

Reflection and Activation:

1. Identify Your Current Battle Zone. Where are you facing the greatest resistance? Name it. Pray over it. Ask the Holy Spirit to reveal what's behind the scenes.

2. Declare Your Assignment. Write down one area you know God has called you to lead in. Begin declaring His Word over it daily. Make prayer your preparation. Pray through *Ephesians 6:10–18*, and declare God's authority over your assignment.

3. Lead with the Spirit. Start each day by asking the Holy Spirit for direction. Record what He reveals and take one obedient step—no matter how small.

4. Encourage a Fellow Warrior. Who do you know that's fighting a quiet battle? Who are your spiritual allies—people who can pray, encourage, and stand with you? Reach out. Pray with them. Remind them: they're not alone.

5. Scripture passages to meditate on:

> ***Psalm 27:1: "The Lord is my light and my salvation—whom shall I fear?"***
>
> ***Ephesians 6:13: "put on the full armor of God, so that when the day of evil comes, you may be able to stand your ground."***

Final Thoughts

Opposition is inevitable—but it is not undefeatable.

Stephen died with glory on his face.
Emily stood with grace in her voice.
And you—you are rising with purpose in your step.

When the world resists your voice, don't fall silent.
When systems reject your presence, don't walk away.
When the pressure mounts, let your knees hit the floor—
then rise in power.

The crown you carry may be invisible.
But in the Spirit—it gleams.

***"You will be called Repairer of Broken Walls…"** —*
Isaiah 58:12 (NIV)

So stand. Speak. Shine.
You are not here to bow.
You are here to *build*.

As you lead, remember: **the weight of the crown may be heavy, but it's also holy.** It means you've been trusted to carry light into darkness, to lift up those who've been beaten down, and to build what others said was impossible.

Now is not the time to shrink back. It's the time to rise.
You are anointed for this.
You are called for this.
And by God's grace—you will finish well.

Crowned for Servant Leadership

Chapter 8
Waiting on God's Timing

Waiting is one of the most uncomfortable assignments God gives to a leader.

You can feel the promise. You've seen the vision.
But the doors remain shut.
The breakthrough hasn't come.
And heaven seems silent.

It's in these in-between seasons—after the dream but before the fulfillment—that God does His deepest work. The waiting room is not wasted space; it is holy ground. Here, God refines your heart, tests your trust, and prepares you to carry the weight of what's coming.

Joseph and Moses—the dreamer and the deliverer—were both shaped by long, painful delays. But those delays weren't detours. They were divine appointments with purpose.

Joseph's Season of Waiting: Forgotten but Not Forsaken

He had been faithful.
He had resisted temptation.
He had interpreted dreams.
He had done everything right.

And yet—he sat in a cell.

Two years.
That's how long Joseph was forgotten after the cupbearer left the prison and returned to Pharaoh's palace.

Two years of silence.
Two years of questions.
Two years of wondering: *Did God forget me, too?*

"They hurt his feet with fetters, he was laid in irons. Until the time that his word came to pass, the word of the Lord tested him." —Psalm 105:18–19 (NKJV)

In that prison, God wasn't just preserving Joseph. He was preparing him. Healing the wounds of betrayal. Crushing pride. Strengthening his character.

When the day finally came—and Pharaoh summoned him—Joseph didn't walk into the throne room bitter or broken. He walked in **ready**.

Key Insight:

Waiting doesn't just reveal your faith—it develops it. God delays fulfillment to develop the vessel.

Moses: Forty Years in the Wilderness of Obscurity

He once walked the marble halls of Egypt.
Now, he walks behind sheep.

Moses had the pedigree. The education. The zeal.
But not the timing.

When he saw a fellow Hebrew beaten, he stepped in with force—and fled in fear. For forty years, the wilderness became his classroom. No crowds. No accolades. Just solitude, sand, and silence.

"And when forty years had passed, an Angel of the Lord appeared to him in a flame of fire..." — ***Acts 7:30*** (NKJV)

God didn't waste the wilderness. In Midian, Moses learned what Pharaoh's palace never taught: **how to lead with patience, how to wait on God, and how to listen.**

And when the bush burned and the call finally came—he was ready, not because he was confident, but because he was *transformed*.

Key Insight:

God often delays promotion until we're mature enough to carry it with humility.

God's Precision in Preparation

Joseph learned stewardship in Potiphar's house.
He learned resilience in prison.
He learned diplomacy in Pharaoh's court.

Moses learned to lead sheep before leading people.
He learned to navigate the wilderness before guiding a nation through one.

Moses' time in the wilderness was as much about internal transformation as it was external preparation. ***Exodus 3:10*** (NKJV) captures God's commissioning of Moses:

"Come now, therefore, and I will send you to Pharaoh that you may bring My people, the children of Israel, out of Egypt."

Had Moses acted prematurely, he would not have been ready for the enormity of his task. Instead, God used the wilderness to mold him into a leader capable of confronting Pharaoh and guiding the Israelites through their own wilderness journey.

"To everything there is a season, a time for every purpose under heaven." —Ecclesiastes 3:1 (NKJV)

God's timing is never random. Every assignment is preceded by an apprenticeship. Every calling is shaped by hidden seasons.

Don't curse the silence. It's shaping your sound.
Don't despise the delay. It's developing your depth.

Key Insight:

Moses' story reminds us that promotion in God's kingdom is not based on human timelines but on divine preparation. Leadership is not just about skills—it's about the character and faith required to steward God's purposes.

From Small Beginnings to Great Responsibilities
Joseph's journey to power didn't begin in Pharaoh's court. It began in a pit. Then a house. Then a prison. Only after he stewarded each season with excellence did God elevate him to rule.

"He who is faithful in what is least is faithful also in much." —Luke 16:10 (NKJV)

Moses spent forty years leading sheep before he led Israel through the Red Sea. That staff in his hand? It was forged in obscurity before it split the Rea Sea.

Key Insight:

Small beginnings are sacred ground. Your consistency in the unseen qualifies you for what will be seen.

Why the Waiting Hurts – and Heals.
Let's be honest—waiting is painful.
It brings to the surface every wound we'd rather ignore: Rejection. Failure. Shame.

But here's the beauty: **God heals in the waiting.**

He healed Joseph of bitterness, so he could forgive his brothers.
He healed Moses of fear, so he could stand before Pharaoh.

"But those who wait on the Lord shall renew their strength..." —Isaiah 40:31 (NKJV)

God will not place destiny in the hands of an unhealed leader. He will use the wilderness to restore what Egypt stole.

Building Trust and Dependence
Joseph could have grown resentful. Moses could have grown cynical. Instead, they trusted.
They believed that God's delay was not denial.

"Trust in the Lord with all your heart, and lean not on your own understanding..." —Proverbs 3:5–6 (NKJV)

They waited—and in time, they walked into history.

Reflection and Activation:

1. Acknowledge Your Waiting Season. What has God promised that you have yet to see fulfilled? Name it. Write it. Surrender it again in prayer.

2. Assess Your Posture. Are you waiting with bitterness, or with faith? What is God trying to heal or develop in you right now?

3. Be Faithful Where You Are. Identify a "small" responsibility you've been given. Choose to show up with excellence and consistency this week.

4. Journal the Lessons. Reflect on how past delays prepared you for future breakthroughs. How did waiting shape your character?

5. Pray for Clarity, Not Just Breakthrough. Ask God what He's doing *in you* while you wait—not just what He's preparing *for you.*

Final Thoughts

God doesn't waste seasons. He doesn't delay without purpose.

He turned a prisoner into a prime minister.
He turned an exile into a deliverer.

He can turn your waiting into your launching.

So don't rush what God is refining. Don't fight the stillness. Don't despise the process.

He is shaping the kind of leader who won't crumble under the weight of your calling.

"For My thoughts are not your thoughts... so are My ways higher than your ways." —Isaiah 55:8–9 (NKJV)

When the moment comes—and it *will* come—
you'll realize that the waiting wasn't punishment.
It was preparation.

And you'll rise, not just ready...
but refined.

Crowned for Servant Leadership

Chapter 9
The Narrow Path of Servant Leadership

The wide road looks easier.
Fewer sacrifices. More applause. Less resistance.

But the narrow path—the one God calls His servant-leaders to walk—is lined with obedience, surrender, and a daily dying to self.

This path won't always feel noble.
It won't often feel fair.
Sometimes, it will feel lonely.

But it's the only road that leads to eternal impact.

Jesus made this clear in **Matthew 7:13–14** (NKJV): ***"Enter by the narrow gate; for wide is the gate and broad is the way that leads to destruction… Because narrow is the gate and difficult is the way which leads to life, and there are few who find it."***

Few find it—because few choose it.
But those who do?
They carry a glory the world cannot comprehend.

The Path of Sacrifice and Obedience

Obedience sounds simple—until it asks for everything.

It asked Noah to build an ark in the middle of a drought.
It asked Abraham to leave everything familiar.
It asked Jesus to carry a cross.

Obedience on the narrow path is costly. It doesn't just ask for your actions—it asks for your allegiance.

When Noah received God's instructions, there was no storm in sight. No sign that rain would come. Yet he obeyed.

"By faith Noah, being divinely warned... moved with godly fear..." —Hebrews 11:7 (NKJV)

Imagine the ridicule.
The jeers from neighbors.
The long days of building when nothing changed.

But Noah wasn't building for a storm—he was building for a **covenant**. (*Genesis 6:8; Genesis 9*)

Key Insight:

Obedience is not about understanding every step—it's about trusting the One who gave the instructions.

Leading with Selflessness and Willingness

True servant leadership is rarely glamorous.
It often looks like washing feet when you'd rather sit at the table.
Or praying for others when your own heart is broken.
Or showing up, quietly and faithfully, when no one sees.

Jesus, in His most vulnerable moment, knelt in Gethsemane.
Sweating blood.
Feeling the crushing weight of what obedience would cost.

"O My Father, if it is possible, let this cup pass from Me; nevertheless, not as I will, but as You will." —**Matthew 26:39** (NKJV)

He didn't just model power—He modeled surrender.

And that's what the narrow path demands.

Philippians 2:3–4 (NKJV) reminds us:
"Let nothing be done through selfish ambition... Let each of you look out not only for his own interests, but also for the interests of others."

This path is not about self-promotion. It's about **self-denial**. And in that place, you become a vessel of eternal influence.

Key Insight:

Surrender is not weakness—it's the soil where true leadership grows.

The Battle Within the Path

The narrow path will test you.
You'll see others racing ahead on the broad road.
They'll gather followers. Gain platforms. Receive praise.

And you'll wonder... *Is obedience worth it?*
That tension—the ache between calling and obscurity—is where many give up.

But Isaiah offers a promise:

"*Fear not, for I am with you... I will strengthen you.*" —*Isaiah 41:10* (NKJV)

God never sends you alone.
He strengthens your feet to walk where few dare tread.

He lifts your heart when weariness presses in.
He reminds you: *You're not being punished. You're being prepared.*

Samuel's Story: Obedience Over Comfort

Samuel wasn't seeking a platform—he was serving in the temple.
Young. Hidden. Uncelebrated.

But God's voice called him in the night.
Not once, not twice—but three times.
And when Samuel finally recognized the voice, he answered:

"*Speak, for Your servant hears.*" —*1 Samuel 3:10* (NKJV)

God didn't start with an easy assignment.
He asked Samuel to deliver a painful word of judgment to Eli, the man who raised him.

Can you imagine the tension in Samuel's heart?
"God, do I really have to say this?"
"What if he's angry?"
"What if I lose his favor?"

But Samuel obeyed. And that obedience unlocked his prophetic destiny.

He didn't walk the wide road of silence. He took the narrow road of truth.

Key Insight:

The narrow path demands courage—especially when obedience costs you human approval.

Carrying Greater Glory

The end of the narrow path is not despair—it is glory.

"Our light affliction… is working for us a far more exceeding and eternal weight of glory." —2 Corinthians 4:17 (NKJV)

The glory God entrusts to servant leaders is not for display—it's for transformation.
It rests on those who have been refined, who have endured, and who have emptied themselves for His purposes.

This glory doesn't shout—it **shines**.
It doesn't seek credit—it **reveals Christ**.

And the world is desperate for leaders like this.

Reflection and Activation:

1. Check the Road You're On. Are you walking the wide path of ease or the narrow road of obedience? Ask the Holy Spirit to reveal any areas where compromise has crept in.

2. Pray the Prayer of Gethsemane. Write your own "not my will" prayer. Be honest. What cup are you asking God to remove? Then surrender it.

3. Serve in Secret. Choose one act of service this week that no one else sees. Do it for God's glory—not man's praise.

4. Embrace Hard Truths. Like Samuel, is there something God is asking you to say or do that feels uncomfortable? Obey with humility and courage.

5. See the Glory Beyond the Grind. Meditate on *2 Corinthians 4:17*. Ask God to open your eyes to how your current "light affliction" is producing something eternal.

Final Thoughts

The wide road is filled with applause, but it ends in emptiness.
The narrow path? It breaks you. Refines you. Rebuilds you. But in the end—it leads to glory.

"In the world you will have tribulation; but be of good cheer, I have overcome the world." —John 16:33 (NKJV)

Don't resent the narrowness.
Don't mourn what others are chasing.
The narrow road is not your prison—it's your platform.

And when the world sees your life—they won't see effort. They'll see **glory**.

Crowned for Servant Leadership

Chapter 10
Carrying the Weight of Glory

When God entrusts you with influence, He is not handing you a platform—He's placing a crown of weight in your hands.

It is not the weight of fame.
It is not the burden of control.
It is the sacred weight of glory.

To lead in the kingdom of God is to carry His presence—not just publicly, but privately. Not just in the spotlight, but in silence. You carry His heart in your decisions, His holiness in your integrity, and His healing in your service.

Leadership is not just a responsibility. It is a sacred *entrustment*.
And when God chooses a leader, He places His glory in fragile hands—so that all the world may see, *it was never about the vessel.*

The Weight of Responsibility

There's a heaviness that settles over every true servant-leader.

It comes in the quiet moments—when you realize your choices shape the lives of others.
It's in the decisions you make behind closed doors, the counsel you give when no one's recording, the prayers you whisper when no one is watching.

Crowned for Servant Leadership

"To whom much is given, much will be required."
—Luke 12:48 (NKJV)

God doesn't promote for prestige. He promotes for *purpose*.

He calls leaders not to carry people's approval—but to carry their burdens.
To lead is to feel the ripple effects of your influence—and to surrender the outcomes to Him.

Leadership carries a profound responsibility that

God Doesn't Just Call – He Equips

When Moses stood before the burning bush, he didn't feel bold. He felt *inadequate*.

"Who am I, that I should go?" ***—Exodus 3:11***
(NKJV)

But God never affirmed Moses with a pep talk. He answered with a promise:
"I will certainly be with you." ***—Exodus 3:12***
(NKJV)

God doesn't just give vision—He gives **presence.**
That is His leadership guarantee: *You don't walk alone.*

David, too, wasn't handed a crown overnight. He learned leadership in obscurity—fighting lions when no one clapped, writing psalms in the shadow of rejection, worshiping with a sling before he held a scepter.

"The Lord, who delivered me…" —*1 Samuel 17:37* (NKJV)

By the time Goliath fell, David wasn't surprised. He had been equipped in the unseen.

Carrying the Weight of His Glory

In the Old Testament, the Ark of the Covenant represented God's manifest presence. And it wasn't to be carried casually.

Only the priests could bear it—and they had to carry it on their shoulders, not carts. The reason? **God's glory was never meant to be rolled on wheels of convenience.** It had to rest on consecrated shoulders.

"The Levites carried the Ark of God… as Moses had commanded." —*1 Chronicles 15:15* (NKJV)

To lead is to become a carrier of God's glory. And that means leadership is never about personality—it's about **presence.**

Gabriel's Story: The President Who Carried the Glory

Gabriel never dreamed of becoming the president of his country.

He dreamed of peace.
He dreamed of justice.
He dreamed of walking through his neighborhood without fear, hearing laughter instead of sirens, and watching his people rise from poverty, not sink deeper into it.

But somewhere between the burden and the prayer, between the injustice and the vision—God whispered: *You will lead this nation.*

He didn't come from a dynasty. He wasn't backed by powerful elites. He came from a quiet Christian home where faith was not an accessory—it was air. His mother would kneel beside his bed every morning and pray, *"Lord, make him a light in darkness."*

He never forgot those prayers.

A Call the World Tried to Silence

At 30 years old, Gabriel announced his candidacy for president, and the political world laughed.

He was too young. Too inexperienced. Too "idealistic." But behind the scenes, he fasted. He prayed. And he cried out for God's will—not just a victory.

As his campaign gained traction, so did the attacks.
Accusations were fabricated.
Media slander spread like wildfire.
One night, an attempt was made on his life—meant to end both his candidacy and his voice.

As bullets shattered glass, Gabriel hit the ground—unharmed.
And in the silence that followed, he heard a whisper in his spirit:
"You will live, and not die, to declare My glory."

It was never about the seat. It was always about the assignment.

The Burden of Glory and the Weight of the Crown

Gabriel won the election—narrowly, miraculously, and undeniably.
It shocked the media. It stunned the establishment. But the people wept with joy.

He didn't take the oath as a man seeking power.
He stepped into office as a man under a divine mantle.

And he immediately fell to his knees.

In the private presidential chapel, on his first night in office, he prayed aloud:
"Lord, I cannot carry this nation. But I can carry Your glory. Show me how."

Glory in Policy, Glory in Prayer

Gabriel's leadership was not conventional.

He fasted weekly while governing.
He called his cabinet to pray before policy.
He refused bribes. He rebuked corruption.
He walked the halls of government as a priest in a suit.

And God moved.

The crime rate, once over 60%, dropped to nearly zero—
0.06%.
Drug cartels dismantled.
Human trafficking routes disrupted.
Gang leaders converted.

The economy, once strangled by inflation, found breath again.
Jobs were created. Local businesses flourished. Foreign investors returned.
Where fear once ruled the streets, children now played freely.

But Gabriel never took credit.
He stood at podiums and spoke only one name: **Jesus.**

"I did not save this nation," he said once, **"God did. I am simply a vessel."**

The True Cost of Glory

Behind the success was a cross.

Gabriel often woke at 3 a.m. to intercede for the people.
He visited families who had lost children to violence.
He wept over the scars of his nation.
He studied Scripture like strategy, seeking heaven's insight for earthly policies.

"The Ark of God was never meant to be carried carelessly," he once told a room of young leaders. **"The glory of God must rest on consecrated shoulders."**

He was referencing *1 Chronicles 15:15* (NKJV)—a reminder that only the Levites, properly prepared, could carry the Ark.

Gabriel lived that principle.
He believed his platform was not for power, but for

presence. Not to magnify a man, but to host the presence of the **King of Kings.**

A Legacy That Reflected Heaven

By his second term, the nation had changed.
But so had Gabriel.

He no longer sought re-election.
He began raising up new leaders—ones who prayed more than they posted.
He mentored them to lead with brokenness, not ego.

He always said, *"If the people see me, I've failed. If they see Christ, we've succeeded."*

And when the time came to step down, he handed over not just an office—but a legacy.

A legacy not written in policies alone, but in presence.
Not measured in popularity, but in the **weight of glory** he had carried well.

Key Insights from Gabriel's Story:

1. Leadership Is a Calling, Not a Campaign. Gabriel didn't seek power—he responded to purpose. When leadership is born in the presence of God, it transforms nations, not just headlines.

2. The Glory of God Demands Consecration. Like the Levites who carried the Ark, Gabriel led with reverence. The Glory isn't cheap. It rests only where there is humility, integrity, and devotion.

3. Intercession Is Greater Than Ambition. Gabriel's power wasn't in politics. It was in prayer. The transformation of a nation began when one man knelt and asked heaven to intervene.

4. The Weight of Glory Is Heavy—but Holy. It demands emotional strength, spiritual stamina, and personal sacrifice. But it also yields eternal fruit—reconciliation, revival, and righteous rule.

5. God Can Use One Life to Shift History. Gabriel's story proves that when God places His hand on one surrendered leader, no weapon, lie, or threat can stop the move of His Spirit.

Reflection and Activation:

1. Are You Ready for the Weight? Consider your sphere of influence. Have you prepared your heart to carry God's glory—not with pride, but with prayer?

2. Lead From the Secret Place. Set a consistent time this week to intercede over your leadership assignment. Ask God for His heart, not just His hand.

3. Invite Glory Into Governance. Whether in your home, your business, your church, or your community—what policies, practices, or patterns need to shift to make room for God's glory?

4. Like Gabriel, who raised up other leaders, consider who you're mentoring. Are you multiplying glory-carriers or merely managing systems?

5. Declare That God Did It. Reflect on past victories. Were they truly yours—or was it the glory of God working through you? Take time to worship, honor, and publicly testify.

Final Thoughts

Carrying the weight of God's glory is both a responsibility and a privilege. As leaders, we are entrusted with His presence, empowered by His strength, and called to reflect His character in all that we do.

The world needs more Gabriels.
Not just presidents, but pastors, educators, entrepreneurs, mothers, mentors, and movement starters—who will carry God's glory with integrity and fire.

God is still looking for those who won't bow to the crowd but will kneel before the throne.
Who won't chase applause, but will chase His presence.
Who will see leadership not as a crown to wear, but a **cross to carry**.

"We have this treasure in earthen vessels..." —2 Corinthians 4:7 (NKJV)

And when the world watches us lead, may they say:
"Surely, the glory of God has been here."

Crowned for Servant Leadership

Chapter 11
The Fivefold Leader: Fulfilling Your Ministry Mandate

There's a crown God gives not just to carry His presence—but to *equip His people.*

It's not a crown forged in gold or lifted by applause.
It is given to those who carry the **weight of responsibility** for souls, destinies, and the building of the church.

This is the crown of the **fivefold leader**.
Apostles. Prophets. Evangelists. Pastors. Teachers.
Each one a gift from Christ to the Body.
Each one called not to be admired, but to activate.

"And He Himself gave some to be apostles, some prophets, some evangelists, and some pastors and teachers..." —Ephesians 4:11–13 (NKJV)

This mandate demands an unwavering commitment to God's Word, a willingness to embrace challenges, and the vision to lead with innovation that aligns with biblical principles. It also requires balancing the dynamic nature of leadership with a steadfast focus on God's eternal truths.

Innovation Rooted in the Spirit, Anchored in the Word

The modern fivefold leader must walk in **ancient truths with fresh fire**.

This is not innovation for relevance's sake. It is **Spirit-led strategy** that emerges from the Word and responds to the times.

God led Joshua to conquer Jericho with **marching and shouting**.
He empowered Gideon to defeat an army with **a trumpet and a torch**.
Neither strategy made sense—but both revealed **heaven's logic**.

Likewise, fivefold leaders must ask:
"God, what is Your divine method for this moment?"

Today's challenges demand **hearing, not copying**. The fivefold leader listens for heaven's blueprint and aligns their methods to eternal truths.

Key Insight:

Creativity must never outpace Scripture. The future of the Church must be led by those who innovate within the bounds of revelation.

Rightly Dividing the Word of Truth

Paul's charge to Timothy is thunder in the ears of every fivefold leader:

"Be diligent... rightly dividing the word of truth."
—2 Timothy 2:15 (NKJV)

The Greek word *orthotomeō* means *to cut straight*.
In other words: Don't twist it. Don't trim it. Don't preach it for applause—**preach it for alignment.**

This requires study. Reverence. Discernment. It means teaching the full counsel of God—**not just the parts that are comfortable or culturally celebrated.**

Your teaching must lead not just to **inspiration**—but to **transformation**.

Key Insight:

The fivefold leader is called to steward the voice of God with clarity and courage, presenting the Word in power and purity.

A Call to Pioneering Vision

To walk in fivefold ministry is to walk where maps don't exist.

It means launching churches when there's no budget.
Preaching truth when it offends.
Prophesying hope when the soil is dry.
Creating discipleship models that don't fit the mold.

Like Abraham, the fivefold pioneer often hears,
"Go… to a place I will show you." —Hebrews 11:8 (NKJV)

God doesn't always give the whole blueprint—just the next step.
But obedience unlocks expansion.

You must walk by faith, not by familiarity.

Key Insight:

Pioneers don't wait for ideal conditions. They move in divine direction, knowing the land is shaped by the feet that walk in obedience.

Deborah's Legacy: Leadership with Clarity and Courage

In a time of oppression and confusion, **God raised a woman with a sword in one hand and a song in the other.**

Deborah didn't fit the cultural mold.
She wasn't elected—she was *anointed*.

As both prophet and judge, Deborah *heard from God—and moved with authority*.
She summoned Barak and declared the word of the Lord:
"Up! For this is the day… Has not the Lord gone out before you?" —Judges 4:14 (NKJV)

She led from under the palm tree—*a place of peace*—and yet ignited a war of freedom.
She didn't compete. She *completed* the assignment.

She teaches us this:
The fivefold leader must be both **intimate with God** and **bold with people**.

And when she sang her victory song, the refrain was clear:
"When leaders lead… praise the Lord!" —Judges 5:2 (NKJV)

Reflection and Activation:

1. Define Your Mandate. Revisit *Ephesians 4:11–13*. Which office has God called you to walk in? How is He using you to equip and mature the Body?

2. Discern Spirit-Led Strategies. Ask the Holy Spirit for specific, creative blueprints to reach and disciple your people. Write down what He reveals.

3. Study to Cut Straight. Commit to one area of biblical study you've neglected. Dive deep. Prepare to teach not just for clarity—but for transformation.

4. Pioneer with Boldness. Identify one area where God is calling you to break new ground. Step forward with courage—even if you don't yet see the full path.

5. Sing Your Song Like Deborah. Reflect on your most recent victories in the ministry. Give God praise—not just privately, but publicly. Let your leadership inspire others to rise.

Final Thoughts

To walk in fivefold ministry is not to build a brand—it is to **build the Body**.

It is not a spotlight—it is a **sacred stewardship**.
You are a trainer of warriors, a healer of wounds, a voice in the wilderness, a shepherd of the scattered, a teacher of truth.

You are not alone. You are not overlooked. You are **crowned** for this.

Crowned for Servant Leadership

"Whatever you do, do it heartily, as to the Lord and not to men." —Colossians 3:23 (NKJV)

Walk in boldness. Preach in fire. Equip in wisdom.
And when the battle is done and the harvest is gathered, may heaven say:
"Well done, good and faithful servant."

Conclusion: Crowned for Servant Leadership

You are not just called—you are **crowned**.
Not with gold.
Not with applause.
But with the weight of purpose, the fire of calling, and the grace to finish well.

This journey has shown us:

- **Stephen**, who was full of faith and fire
- **Joseph**, refined in the pit and elevated in the palace
- **Deborah**, who heard from God and led with courage
- **Moses**, who wrestled with insecurity but walked in power
- **Gabriel**, the president who rebuilt a nation on prayer
- And ultimately, **Jesus**, the King who washed feet and carried a cross

These are not distant stories—they are **blueprints**. They are **reminders**.
And now, they are your **legacy.**

To be crowned for servant leadership is to:

- Embrace the narrow road
- Carry the weight of His glory
- Lead with truth and tenderness
- Equip others to go further than you

- And reflect Christ in every decision

Let His words echo over you even now:
"You were faithful over a few things; I will make you ruler over many. Enter into the joy of your Lord." —Matthew 25:21

So lead with honor.
Serve with joy.
And carry your crown—not as a trophy, but as a trust.

Because this world doesn't need more heroes.
It needs more servants... **crowned by the King to finish the work.**

Prayer for the Finishers

A Prayer for the Finishers

Heavenly Father, we come before You, lifting up every present-day Stephen—those You have called and crowned for such a time as this. For too long, the enemy has whispered lies, declaring they start but do not finish. But today, we reject that lie from the pit of hell! These chosen ones are not quitters; they are *finishers*.

In the mighty name of Jesus, we cancel every negative word spoken over their lives by friends, family members, coworkers, or anyone who has tried to hinder Your purpose in them. We declare, "Get behind them, Satan! You are an offense to the plans of God." Your schemes shall no longer prevail. Every seed of destruction you've planted is uprooted, and every curse spoken is null and void. Those words shall fall to the ground, never to rise again, for the Lord Himself has declared victory over His finishers!

Father, we decree and declare that each of Your chosen vessels will complete the assignments You have placed before them. Let the finishers arise with boldness, strength, and unwavering faith. Let every enemy of their purpose be scattered. In 2025 and beyond, we proclaim no more interference by the enemy. Your army, O God, shall stand united, pushing back every force of darkness that has encroached upon their homes, families, and endeavors.

Lord, rebuild what has been torn down. Let the walls of their spiritual and physical foundations be restored—stronger, deeper, and more secure than ever before. Pour out Your virtue and provision upon them, giving them all they need to thrive. Let the tools of the Kingdom be placed in their hands, and may they wield them with skill, precision, and anointing to accomplish Your work in this season.

Thank You, Father, for Your divine protection, Your abiding presence, and Your righteous judgment over all evil. As Your chosen ones, we take our rightful place, clothed in the full armor of God, ready to war a good warfare. We stand strong, firm, and victorious, for the battle belongs to You, Lord.

In Jesus' mighty name, we pray. Amen.

About the Author

Dr. Lisa Michelle Vice carries the fire of a prophet, the wisdom of a teacher, and the heart of a servant-leader. Her journey began not on a stage—but in the prayer-saturated home of a faith-filled family in the South Bronx, where the echo of revival was the soundtrack of her childhood.

She is the great-granddaughter of a tent revivalist and the granddaughter of a prophetic intercessor whose prayers still ripple through generations. Her father sang over congregations with holy conviction, while her mother laid theological foundations as a Sunday school teacher. Lisa, the quiet child at the piano, didn't yet know she was being trained to carry the weight of God's glory.

At just five years old, she performed at **Carnegie Hall** and **Town Hall** in New York City. But her greatest stage was the altar, where at age ten, she had a life-changing encounter with the Holy Spirit that marked her with a hunger for God she could never shake.

As a teenager growing up amidst the gritty challenges of urban life—violence, addiction, and brokenness—Lisa chose purity, purpose, and prayer. At eighteen, she escaped a house fire with her toddler daughter in what she calls a divine rescue that cemented her conviction: **God was not finished with her life. He was just beginning.**

She would go on to marry her childhood sweetheart and travel across the U.S., Germany, and Korea as a military spouse—carrying not only her family, but the gospel. In 1987, another powerful encounter with God shifted everything. Thirty years later, she was publicly anointed as a prophet—a moment that confirmed what heaven had already written.

Dr. Lisa Vice believes prophets aren't made—they are born. And they are born for *assignments*.

Over nearly four decades, she has served, trained, mentored, through the lens of **holiness, character, and purity**. She holds a **Doctorate in Christian Theology**, a **Bachelor's in Prophetic Ministry**, and is the former president of **Arise International School of Ministry**. She's also the voice behind the *Carry His Glory Now* podcast—a global platform equipping listeners to lead with power, purity, and prophetic precision.

Beyond the pulpit, she's been a **small-business owner**, a **retired U.S. Postmaster**, and a **managerial leader** in multiple spheres—all while raising a family and walking in the rhythm of prayer and purpose.

Her life is a prophetic tapestry—woven with survival, submission, and sacred fire.

Now, through her writing and ministry, **Dr. Lisa Vice carries one mandate:**
To crown a generation of servant-leaders who will walk in their God-given authority, carry His glory without compromise, and transform the world for His name.

She doesn't just teach leadership. She **lives it**.

And her prayer is that you will too.

Crowned for Servant Leadership

Crowned for Servant Leadership

Crowned for Servant Leadership

Other Resources: eBooks link:

https://payhip.com/admingemministryorg

Crowned for Servant Leadership

Continue your journey of transformation with these paperback resources: **The Message of Purity, God's Way – Revised Edition**, its companion **Activation Workbook** and **Facilitator's Workbook**—tools designed to deepen your

understanding, inspire growth, and equip you for the weight of God's greater glory.

Scan the QR Code to access:

Crowned for Servant Leadership

Crowned for Servant Leadership

Crowned for Servant Leadership

Crowned for Servant Leadership

---

[1] Habakkuk 2:14 - For the earth shall be filled with the knowledge of the glory of the LORD, as the waters cover the sea.
[2] Isaiah 60:2 - For, behold, the **darkness** shall cover the earth, and **gross darkness** the people: but the LORD shall arise upon thee, and his glory shall be seen upon thee.
[3] Philippians 2:5 - Let this mind be in you, which was also in Christ Jesus.
[4] Acts 6:8 - And Stephen, full of faith and power, did great wonders and miracles among the people.
[5] Acts 2:4 - And they were all filled with the Holy Ghost, and began to speak with other tongues, as the Spirit gave them utterance.
[6] Acts 4:8 - Then Peter, filled with the Holy Ghost, said unto them, Ye rulers of the people, and elders of Israel,
[7] Acts 6:3, 5, 8 - Wherefore, brethren, look ye out among you seven men of honest report, full of the Holy Ghost and wisdom, whom we may appoint over this business. (5) And the saying pleased the whole multitude: and they chose Stephen, a man full of faith and of the Holy Ghost, and Philip, and Prochorus, and Nicanor, and Timon, and Parmenas, and Nicolas a proselyte of Antioch: (8) And Stephen, full of faith and power, did great wonders and miracles among the people.
[8] Acts 13:9 -Then Saul, who was also called Paul, filled with the Holy Spirit, looked straight at Elymas and said,
[9] Micah 3:8 - But as for me, I am filled with power, with the Spirit of the LORD, and with justice and might, to declare to Jacob his transgression, to Israel his sin.
[10] 1 Samuel 1:10-11 - In her deep anguish Hannah prayed to the LORD, weeping bitterly. (11) And she made a vow, saying, "LORD Almighty, if you will only look on your servant's misery and remember me, and not forget your servant but give her a son, then I

Crowned for Servant Leadership

---

will give him to the LORD for all the days of his life, and no razor will ever be used on his head."

Made in the USA
Coppell, TX
12 April 2025

48237944R00066